Fire & Ice

Nine Poets from Scandinavia and the North

edited by
Gordon Walmsley

translations by
Bernard Scudder
Gordon Walmsley
Didda

salmonpublishing

Published in 2004 by Salmon Publishing,
Cliffs of Moher, County Clare, Ireland
web: www.salmonpoetry.com
email: info@salmonpoetry.com

Paperback ISBN 1 903392 37 3

A CIP record for this title is available from the British Library.

The publisher gratefully acknowledges the financial assistance of Helge Fonden and Balder Fonden towards the publication of this book.

Cover Artwork: Stein Mehren
Cover Design & Typesetting: Siobhán Hutson
Printed in Ireland by Colour Books

For Jessie Lendennie

who was awake to this thought:
that the rainbow of the north should touch the green island

Acknowledgements

It isn't always one is able to work in congenial quarters on an island as lovely as Gotland, Sweden. For that privilege I am grateful to the Baltic Centre For Writers and Translators, where I lived for a month at the commencement of this mammoth project, the result of which is this small book. I would especially like to thank Lena Pasternak and Gerda Helena Lindskog who have the knack of creating an atmosphere absolutely perfect for writers and those who recreate texts from one language to another. And I would like to thank a Swedish translator I met in Gotland for wise words that have guided me through this project. "It must be difficult to translate writers who think they know English," he said to me one day. And then, "In the end only you can be the judge, because though they may be very good at English they can't hear the nuances you can." I have followed this advice. Carefully. Very carefully. And thus all faults are ultimately mine. I would also like to thank people who helped me check the texts, Marta Alsvåg, Inger Lise Oehlrich, Manni Koestler. As I say, none are responsible for errors of judgement or of translation. They did their best and sometimes I did not take their advice.

I would also like to thank Scandinavia and the North for giving us these writers. And for Patience, Time and Space. Without these three beings the project would never have been successfully completed.

And thanks of course to Helge Fonden & Balder Fonden for supporting *Fire and Ice*.

g.w.

Contents

Foreword

"Unless you have been / both in Heaven and Hell/ I don't believe your word" is the inscription Willum Peder Trellund uses to preface one of his collections.

They are lines each of these poets might punctuate with a nod of the head.

Each has, one feels, experienced a just portion of darkness and light. Each has felt the cold breath in the night, the pivotal moment.

Thus they know the mood of the threshold, the place where light casts our shadows.

The world of the north, of Scandinavia and the islands, is a world in which the veil between seen and unseen worlds has its very own quality of transparency. This quality has its pendant in what we call intuition. That the people of the European north have for centuries been esteemed for intuitive qualities should come as no surprise to the readers of these poems.

Where but in Iceland could there exist a special department of the government, whose task is to confer with elemental beings who might be disturbed by building or highway projects? Everyone knows the story of the highway near Reykjavik that was to plough through a massive rock. Yet the beings of the rock protested. And so the highway was rerouted...

Moving across the threshold.

Sometimes it is tentative, a groping. Language then becomes a sensory organ touching the contours of worlds.

Sometimes the movement is a decisive stride.

In moving between the two worlds, the seen and the unseen, each of these poets conducts an act of exploration. And what characterizes them is that they, through the sensings of the poetic word, want to share their experiences with us. The wish to tell us what they have found.

Sometimes it is a fragmentary groping...
Sometimes it is a sharing of a struggle with demons and angels...
Sometimes it is a sensing...

Each of these poets has immense courage. That will become clear to readers as they make their way through this book. The processs of fashioning poems is a process of fashioning the individuals who write them.

Through fire and ice.

GORDON WALMSLEY
Copenhagen 2004

Katarina Frostenson
(Sweden)

from *Joner*

We Resemble

We resemble one another. There is hardly any difference.
Tonight. In the light of moon child. We are laid up side by
side, linen stacked on white tables of wooden legs. This is a
night with no one sleeping. A quiet assembly, scents of the
common sleeping room in the air. In lengths of lanky holbein's
christ. What kind of a silence wishes to make its presence
known. What kind of features are at rest. How white
everything fundamentally looks. Suitably so. Fundamentally.
Everything. Resembling. *Draws near* A smile ignites—moves
as a blue flame over the whole row, it spreads and vanishes.
The cold fixes You-Who-Are-Observing take one step back
Back away There are features smiling at you

stroked across features lustring
voice ashatter, gravel-dashed

vessels of murmuring, dark, unprobed
sounds   resound

Negative, Twinkle

Someone resembling me
someone who resembled me, to the very end
so the verb stops walking

Evil is your own rhythm—there is none in things.
Sounds   resound—
to stride through the world resounding

your forehead wrestling with things. To be: against. No.
No.—No name. Things resembling, and few words. "I want to"—
And then silence

the curtain rises. Folds descend.
The coverlet tumbles on down, over—the world
is here: that's the upshot

once and for all—a string of pearling days
What is to be done with this Ever-Revealing-Lucid
phantomnal bulwark...

I stalk the border   World
I will hound you to the rim
Where the membrane of images bursts, where features slacken

are flayed, divulged, in sun-cleansed visage
from the entrails of the face...I am jolted by my own thoughts
my thoughts, a roaming beast drifting in sunlight

clear, clearer, clearest
what is there within—I want to root it out, there where the
brow creases. And then listen—pellucidly murmurous

I lie upon the hill, receiving the sun
I dream of clear things, things resounding, that strike
one another: *to be there within*

The clear world gets up again. *You should*
shadow the world, follow close in its tracks. Mimic it
into the vanishings

enter into the figure hovering the city.
The only one. Silent. Like the
Cloud. yes—

morning over hills of the city. Eggshell and sun
I cry towards the borderlands! My dream visage following along
Strewn with wax. White eyelids—shading

calm, faintly smiling. It smiles
so dark. It smiles so dark and peevish the egg
I want it now

I want to defile it with my pin, cast it out. I want to
force its expression from its frame: what do you want, really
To dissect a smile

like two men
like two men who came. Who saw. Who stood listening
over the round table's gleam. A body's many parts

there is no sated fullness in the eye
no raw
there is no root within crying out

no—defence. What is this pursuit of parts internal in all things
see, the mechanism, that which hides there within
darkness, the trembling pupa...

pain shoots down my long unhealed wound, blinding negatively
take out the cold; illumine it for a long time and well: This smiling
black egg the world is hatched into

that which resembles me   the sham grin of the enshrouded one
a shiny visage. Resonance, a high firm brow
A beam

from another…Can you see all things from some other quarter
can you make a full turn around. Trade it in, choose
some other point of view, perspective—

No, you idiot, this isn't a question of taste!
no "something else". Behind your forehead
beyond the gate, within the grove, hidden there—

is only the great, shadowless effigy
Thou art placed against   world called
once and for all

you can turn, around
you can crush the form
you can always obliterate your own peevishly constructed form

all—into nothing. That freedom exists where you stand. Listen to
your voice speak. A black plastic rag flies up over your mouth (this
world's emblem, cold sign mocking) You stand, moving your mouth

you continue to speak. Yes, speaking is a wandering thing
The verb will probe on through to the heart till it stops
all that flows. And yet. Here, now. And until further notice. Nothing

stops it: so you stand there, your back exposed. Smile,
sicken, grow accustomed to the light: to what is taking place
you no longer mind

I shine like a star
I am lucid

Don't look around.
You are turned. Already

why do you look
so grey

in the rain of spikes

the wound's lip

from *Korallen (The Coral)*

Tempest

A bone, the colour of toffee,
drifting on water, edging the cove,
I follow it, watching. Flurries

through the air. Tree drawing itself on a cheek
network of veins, red. I think of a dream-
I dreamt someone was saying I didn't live

reverberating night words. Did they seize me
between the sheets. The stiff leaves—say
when did I get to be dead

dead. dead. dead. staring towards the ceiling
The question is repeated, warm water of the tap in my mouth—
chair-back to the chin, streaks of blood on the wall

another dream drifted up towards the bed, about
numbness, the urge to be loosened from bones, frame
lifted out of the body. There was the feeling

of a husk. Leaning against a tree trunk
like a black double,
placed on the cold ground like a statue

an Alsatian sniffs among the reeds,
scruffy here among the grasses, orange peels, auburn leaves,
Nose knocking the frozen earth

the wind blows cold round the island out there
the cove's reedy island: see the yellow grass bending
somehow abandoned in the water's midst

at the entrance to the park it comes towards me, the
island and the phrase: *animals under island*, cast to the ground
before our feet. Written in the grey gravel. It was there. Still

don't be alarmed by that spectral revenant, he is the very heart of the arts
An inscription, somewhat staid within the image, frozen in,
inlaid—I seek what moves within the frozenness

waves within glass—it was in January
I stood before the gate, waiting
A man was walking across the meadow

who is it is walking through the ancient grasses, a shape
clad in brown, dragging his foot behind him
silver clapper of a shoe striking the stones

I hear a clanging, and its echo, the janglings
of metal—the Alsatian has
found out the bone, sees it gliding out towards the island

Only its keening sense stirs, the nose aquiver
Such a pure and elemental terror. *I want it!*
The red tree on the cheek grows, bursts

cold, says the child, cold, cold everywhere
How cold it is: I'm freezing from a silence like cinders
in a room that has been closed off. *Father.* I think

I swallowed my voice—as the genii in the bottle
it lives somewhere—out there, perhaps it lives
among the hills in the park. Thinking

of that Lenz, who walked among mountains in January, walking
through valleys, allowing his voice to open. The movement
came back—a closure for an opening

That was in January, the month of partition
of severity, Saturn, the guardian of the threshold
who is austere and yet creative in his austerity

it was in this time of dearth when the voice presses
into the sap, birds strangled in song, like it
the voice will soon explode into the air. Blue and steel-like cold

a father hand, a father fount and it must
be cold. That is the way of the fount—Hermione
suddenly thinks. *Hermione's speech.*

and warmth emerging from another larynx. Wind pipe—A man
ascends the stairs to the temple of echoes, slow and cautious
with the circumspection such steps demand here

tumbles back, slips on an ice patch
Do I hurl myself forward then or do I just look, out—
A lovely bow hovers in the air—

A humanbow and the cry
Tells me most quietly that this is taking place out there
Out there—and what is it called—you can look

at almost anything at all, observe it at
a distance without blinking and
with no terror

hardly a sound, no word here, only
the Swedish way of moving the mouth, down-turned
to avert what in a word may threaten

I have dreamed this land, seen it
as a tiny box with few small signs upon it, growing smaller
day by day, a shrivelling alphabet

one night I walked through an avenue of placards
three words covering the land, out by that shorn brink
far from any red cock's-comb crest where voices

hack and kill—Speech
I feel grief, like the living dead
as if someone were to breathe over you, to waken you

into life…a fervent kiss to the brow, breathing
downward, toward the skull, bone…lowering you down towards
that which braces, listen—

the refrain, all of them…The silvery ringing,
quiet water, the snipe's complaint, the child's warm tear,
the cold

night, a cold snap, the popped string, "Here we go round
the mulberry bush the mulberry bush"—the thought
like a small hole there for rags and beasts, colours

all the languages that gather. Celestial lightness
sound of root, croakings, words clashing together
to a howl—that sound of hunger

the dark plummet will be fastened to
a tree, to the trunk, sinking
towards the root neath the earth where it sings

rip 'em, shove 'em, drive 'em up then
deep down under—Echo across the park, a pennant
yellow atop the skyscraper by the gate, smell of iron in the air

the dog has vanished, the bone is out there…the island
is calm, sees the faint gleam below…come to the sands
by water's edge, come to the park's strange longing, to

this ocean of the world on the brink. It is at a distance you
see them, hear again that ringing, the ragamuffin bunch
making its way under water, listen

a wave, a hammer
striking stone, a coral strange
and languorous from the ground's deep

NOTE: *animals under island*. alternatively, *animals under [the letter]* ö.

Lene Henningsen

(Denmark)

thoughts on poetry...

First the questions.
If the time can be grasped. With words.
If every place has its transformation,
the future giving warning, opening up
the transformations. With words.
If what is new demands this: Now
/transcendence/ leap. If so.
Then let me be the most extreme
example. Poem.
How to bear the world/ knowledge that increases
intractable/ reckless speech in the nerves'
electrical vegetation.
Eternal questions, eternal responsibility,
the need for meaning. Deeper, deeper.

How to be one with the world/paradoxes
contradictions/impossibilities/depth
voices and always more voices.
Bounding onto speeding trains:
From beauty into loss and pain.
With visible or invisible violence
until lust and waters of the mouth flow over
screens and invisible chains.
How to fathom/enlighten/explain
what is seen.

No capitulation. No compromises.
In the poem: No guide. No dictator.
In the world, unfamiliar pictures congregate
seeking to contrast/illumine/become a gleam
in the aggregate.
Rhythms and tones are drawn from earth and air
in celestial—terrestrial dialogue.
Space is permitted to unfold. Tell the one who
listens: be my guest, come along, follow
your ways.
The globe draws the map. Notice
the dancer, the singer, the fairy-tale adventurer.
They tell the tale of a face.
Entering into existence.
Similar to magic. Which occurs.
Divides the space once more.

·

The rite can have the appearance of a circle of crosses
united with the sun. Life-cross. The sun's jewel
to the earth.
Try again, travel through, dazzling/subtle
night-morning, night-morning.
A ritual is lived through, knows no
heed, perhaps it takes it. Requires strength/
will/blood. Gives back life.
The rite is a program for writing poetry
that cannot be programmed. Investigates
what the real can bear. How strong
a sun the universe can bear. The attempt
is symbol and reality.
I say. I live. And it is *one*
breath.

·

Music leads the way. Music leads me.
I will travel anew/send myself
off/give new names to the countries.
(Notice a glance without trepidation).
Rip open and grasp in advance, peer into the clouds/
the fire of a future time. A future time requests
words and obtains them. Belongs to the clouds/
to the fire. Puts things behind and accepts.
It is that alone. The raw attempt.
The song that wishes to be deepened.
(Incurable anger? Give me
delight in an incision as clear as lightning
turning the entire tale topsy-turvy. The glance
that *is* ardour.

Song. The singer. Go deeply in/without fear/
unfathomable. Grasp the shadows, the flickering
remnants of the tale, delicate threads
among the living, between the living and
the dead.
In the end only the fire. Can be found here.
Is able to return. Thin layers of
black and white ashes. Begin here. A glance
that meets. That is the miracle's ever-revolving
joker. The only one necessary. Now.

•

(Silence. shall we leave it alone?)

From silence through a landscape never seen,
though inhabited. From roads through a
landscape never driven through, although known.
Someone waits for words and hears them.
Granting, once again, silence.
Final stop before the border. Guards
expect nothing. They hand out papers, smoking,
and they speak as if time had simply
run down.
One moment. And there is the first station in
the realm of invisibility. Movement takes over:

What is it I know about? I think, dream.
Later, death. You place upon the silence a
circle of flames. Shaping the fire/
gathering the world into a glance.
When everything acquires heat. I will give myself
to the darkness.

poems…

Winter Song

Let me fold something white
as a rose to you
longing like me

The paper leaps up
ready for the next slice

I maintain
there is nothing of penance in this
that I'm not just up for anything

What is written will avenge itself
will grow smaller and smaller
a trivial stain in the end to our eyes

Hahaha
the night of the knives
more than small lies

take care of the dreams
white beasts may have:

Trembly impossible longing
lacerated beauty
the kind we see in one another

breath icing-up on its way away
it can just as well be
in this night of tales

Short Cut To The North Wind

Short cut to the north wind
I take your hand
I loosen the cold into the smallest of threads
I think of a journey only now begun
I don't know if you're coming to a standstill
I turn my face towards your unknown face
My hand strokes a sleeping child
I lean back and pick up a rusty can
I assess the transformation
It turns into water and voices
Short cut to the north wind
I paint the hills green underneath
I hold two stories within me with fissures and stains
I don't call a fissure an abyss
I don't call a stain blindness
I leap over hell with my eyes bound
I'm willing to leap, to leap for life
My hand strokes a sleeping child
I have learned as one who gathers chestnuts and cones
I haven't seen it as a question of learning
I don't know who has made the best use of me
I assume it is God
I wish for everyone a promise that can't be broken
I see our moment as the greatest chance
Short cut to the north wind
I suppose I can respect the wisdom of it

My hand strokes a sleeping child

I wish everyone might touch a word's blood sky

I wish everyone might love until the white winter of vanishings

I lean back, way way back

I dream of homes all aflower

I take your hand

I write the word you instead

Underground

I

What you never observed
                Flew with the ash and it was
                        What you knew
This evening

This evening
Some power is sweeping the city
A land will become aware of it in one night
A land will increase in one night
That was   What you knew

And since nothing can contain everything
You will lean even further out you will
                Sink under and leave behind you will
                Worship
                Unsparingly
                        When all of you are dreaming

                        Lucid silhouettes
                        Created alone
During the night
During a hard-sought nuance of light

It is alone   A choice of transforming

II

You knew
You were to sail with lights
                    Through the impossible

You have no knowledge of the sea?
                    Evil flotsam resembling lost streets
                                        At night
                    Lanterns suggesting an arena fully-rigged
There is a cry and a warning
                    Simple
There is only one thing to choose

While the eagle builds his nest
                    Wings spanning heaven and earth
Could it be
You are contemplating a change into air?
                    Or the skin of some sacrificial beast
Could it be that it is too late?

You know   here
Wings are the providence of man

Fire clings
        Always clings
Asking only—
voice of an eagle in your hair:

What should be left behind?

III

And when you are moving deeply, you can ask yourself
Dissolve a fever

              Hoarse and cold

              In your blood

Timepieces will slowly crumble
Into day
Do you wish to turn back?

Because look you climb

              Your smile painting us into blackness

              We can write out the final notes
Fly through your brow with no pain
Become and we can become

Dome of night   Sight of wing   That look

Was expected for so long   A prayer of soot

              To ravage your heart

              The drumming of death   free
       From the gloom of a levity that is white
       This

                       And more

A moonchild is born and walks by your side
Pushing the world's stroller into

All things   In a jumble   Lights readjusted   Relinquished

Thus we drew

    Sand through a black sea

        Built ten bright walls   and stood up

Passenger

Only now is the city we walk into
A clenched fist transformed
Only now is the street changed into a harbour
A windy song, the coughing of a demi-god
Only now is the cry flailing
Us through, long since a ship
Only now is it under full sail
The space filled with flames of nothingness
Only now does the night borrow hope from the night
Veering towards the wind, allowing us to live
Only now do we fold together what we have decided
The breadth of all things is deeper than the sea
Mix a cough or sweetest malts
With the sound: a heart long since under way

Einar Mar Gudmundsson
(Iceland)

Homer the singer of tales

One rainy afternoon,
on a ship from a much-travelled dream,
Homer the singer of tales arrived in Reykjavík.
He walked from the quayside
and took a cab that drove him
along rain-grey streets
where sorry houses passed by.

At the crossroads Homer the singer of tales turned
to the driver and said:
"How can it be imagined
that here in this rain-grey
monotony lives a nation of storytellers?"
"That's exactly why," answered the cab driver,
"you never want to hear
a good tale as much as when the drops
beat on the windows."

When the drops beat on the windows
and the fog gliding into the bay
covers mountain and ocean alike,
nothing worth the telling
except the slush on the streets,

no enchanting song,
no singing sun,
only footprints that vanish
like rain into the ocean,
into the void and the wind
that sings and blows...

Cloaked in grey
time passes along the streets,
the odd bird hovers

dreamlessly above the town,
the clouds' veils of rain
tighten around the throat
and the dark of night pours
like a net over the world.

A man sails a boat out into the ocean,
there is a singing wave,
there is a sleeping house,
a sail wrung in a dream,
the world ripples
across a black sea
and the lights pass
like flames along the streets.

Brushstrokes of blue

And the ocean ...

where the Almighty mirrors his countenance
blind as the soul's waves, crashing,
choppy, with grey dreams in their arms
and exotic words on their lips.

When the sun floats at the ocean's rim
the island is lit up in a blaze
ice cubes of peaks
glasses full of glowing wines.

A canvas stretched over the world
and framed with cliffs,
a mirror in a salty drop
squawking birds and rocks.

．

See the brushstrokes,
how they ripple through the world,
blue in a singing wave
words thrashing like fish.

And the foam ...
like the beard of an old man
who steps ashore and vanishes in the ocean,
the dark ocean, the billowing sea.

．

Moon-glade rocking on the waves
a black fiddle with a curl of cloud,
a dance to a musty stick
and breakers from an old dream,

relics of an old herring jetty
or high-seat pillars of yore ...
This island is a floating shield
with rock stacks standing up like spears.

.

And the ocean ...

now it rises from the shore
and walks into the village
wearing a coat of grey fog,
snatches the children into its arms
leads them by the hand down the street
over a fence of dreams
yellow puddles that ripple,

leads them by the hand
with singing blue in its eyes
then lies down beneath the cliff
and rests in the rock
to the accompaniment of squawking birds.

.

Like the spring of life in a dream
in the black hole of night
in the mausoleum of drowning winds
your route lies uncharted through the world

When they walk away
there is still upwelling beneath their soles,
the brushstrokes of the world
the blue of thrashing words.

A Farewell to Arms

This is the cliff ...

On this cliff
the empire built a military base.
Land was settled with helicopters,
radar telescopes, buildings and weapons,
everything that befits
a military base on the rim of the world.
Yet it soon became clear to all
that the task was hopeless,
that the cliff could not be threaded
on to the chain of the age
that now enclosed the world.
But there was no stopping:
the base's construction had to be finished.
And it would be operated
with the main aim
of abandoning it again.

This is the cliff ...

the cliff
where old chart-toppers
glide among empty houses
and the fog opens a door
into unknown worlds.
On the floor, a glacier sits
talking in its sleep
of rusty relics
from the empire of time,
ancient ice ages
and an eternal wait for nothing.

This is the cliff ...

the cliff
where an abandoned
radar dish lies in the fog
sleeping without contact
with the world

and books
full of cracked codes
from a long-forgotten war
are buried in snow

the cliff
where gliding days chart
the wastes of time
that remained behind
when the soldiers left.

This is the cliff ...

on this cliff they roamed
in loneliness and silence,
in the fog of northern gloom
and darkness thick as wool,
through emptiness so deep and dim
that in droves they walked
off the cliffs and perished
in the darkness of this land,
in the emptiness behind time
where the cliff stands
in the swelling surf
and the winter climbs mountains.

Hauntings

I

The weather is cold
and the countryside sad
and dim to behold.

Word arrives
of hauntings in the valley
of winds blowing
and winter besieging
hills and moors.

The weather is cold
weird shadows abroad
the walls whine
and hailstones rage
in waves over meadows.

A booming voice,
deep as the darkness
vanishes into the black
and the howling blizzard.

Someone asks
where he is
but no one can answer,

tinder falls into fire,
nothing is visible
but drifting snow.

II

The weather is cold,
dim to behold,
sad in the shadowed valley.

When day breaks
a bloody trail is seen
up to the cliff.

Sheep have been killed
or strayed to the mountains,
walkers are bowed in greyness

—the evil-doer has vanished—

but he lies silent,
heavy as a bull,
his hair grey as a wolf's,
icy darkness in his eyes.

III

The weather is cold,
the clouds swoop
like birds about the moon,
weird shadows abroad.

Below is the world
naked and grey,
the night chilly...
he can be seen
walking around the farm.

From the icy darkness
a glowing terror stares,
behold the man,
lying broken there,
every bone smashed apart.

Beneath a shadow from the mountain
emptiness passes over the meadow.

IV

Around the door
everything is broken and smashed,
cold winds pierce
through the rooms and walls.

Only a tiny single light,
a door like a wedge
and the beds all in disarray
over a deserted stage
the clouds flap like a curtain.

He clambers up the buildings
and straddles the farmhouse,
its foundations creak,
his head towering
like a rough-hewn cliff.

The struggle spreads
like wildfire,
flickering curtains
over a deserted stage,
in icy darkness
the moon gleams like a blaze.

The Eye of Chaos

Do not talk about
large nations and small nations,
outposts, corners and peripheries.

This is a globe; its centre
rests beneath your feet
and shifts its ground and follows
you wherever you go.

Inger Christensen

(Denmark)

Light

I

I know once again
a glade in the language
the words that are closed
are there so you love them
repeating on in to what's simple—
A swan that will fold itself up
round an egg
is ever an echo
of genesis in us
And the swan that will fly
your eye towards the sun
is ever again
prophetically wondrous

You can in the word
know again light
the baffling ways
of a man to a woman
And the word that can change
your mind to a swan
is simple enough
to form a small egg
And language that closes
itself in an egg
has wings that will carry
from birth into light
And the sun that is there to be loved

II

I think of a sun
of a swan and of madness
of matter that brightens
with no matter in it
swinging unbridled
a lantern of chance
so physical a miracle
is a light
when eternity condenses
draws near
and doesn't kill

I think of a mask
and a marbling sun
a cloak of feathers
and white brain mass
—May death be as cold—
I think of a wonder
the heart as a lantern
swaying by chance
between this I
and nothing at all
in madness and light

III

I think a light
that the sun is much stronger
soberly grasping
the body's free-fall
and swirling flakes
of light all around it

I think a promise
in keeping with pureness
and that light has provided us
wings that are stronger
than even the sun's in its space
to die in

And besides this, a body
faintly illumined
by uncertain promise
yet never a wall
and only this constant:
I think a light

IV

The thing about growing
is maybe the same
I think of a tree
of a bird and of fantasy
and beyond all bridling
wings will write
the growth of a dream
And where you fell
sleep has provided
other deep places
to open the winds
from what was ripped loose

I think of a sorrow
and where it has fallen
the bird has again
hung up a nest
big as the heavens
my mind for to live in
The thing about growing
is maybe the same
as living a dream
No sorrow can hinder
bird and fantasy

V

Repeat into me
that this is enough
that this is the body's
own smoking light
that this is right now

Dust holds no
desperate echo
our only life
is a rose of life
that we love

Repeat to me darling:
the lantern you're swinging
so soundlessly round me
is ever again
a child just beginning

I Write As The Wind...

I write as the wind
that writes with a clouds'
quiet script

or speeds through the skies
in vanishing strokes
as by swallows

I write as the wind
writing in water
stylised monotonous

or rolling with waves'
thumping alphabet
foamy threads

writing in air
as plants that are writing
with stalks and with leaves

or round as a flower's
circles and wisps
dots and small threads

I write as a stretching beach front
writes–in a fringe
of shellfish and kelp

or delicate, fine, as mother–of–pearl
starfish feet
and mussel slime

I write as the early most
spring writes
anemones' beech trees'
violets' and the forest lilacs'
common alphabet

I write as the childish
summer that thunders
carapaces by forest's edge
as gold that is white when lightning
grows great with wheatening fields

I write as doomed
autumn would write
thrashing hope
as a light storm pierces
misty remembrance

I write as winter
writes like snow
or ice and cold
and gloom and death
write

I write as a heart
that is beating writes
the skeleton's nail's
teeth's hair's
and the cranium's hush

I write as a heart
that is beating writes
the hands' feet's
skin's lip's
and sex's whisper

I write as a heart
that is beating writes
the lungs' muscles'
face's brain's
and nerves' sound

I write as a heart
that is beating writes
the blood's and cells'
sight's weeping's
and the tongue's cry

from *alphabet*

There's something so special
    the way that doves
        live out my life
            as were it their due

today when it rains
    and always when raining
        they softly alight
            on the house's sill

so close to this white
    sheet of paper
        they can easily see if I write
            about doves or the rain

it can feel somehow wrong
    that it never is doves
        who quiet in mind
            write about doves

or even the rain
    or panes in a window they peep
        through in blurs to me
            with a little round eye

they don't even know
    that especially in flying
        wings are linked
            to silken peace

a state of affairs nearly
    doomed to failure
        calling doves merely doves
            in for instance a poem

or even doves in the rain
    as the tousled sopping wet
        doves-in-the-rain they are
            today when it's raining

the first time was really
    in Berlevågs harbor
        where gulls ever rail
            in the chill of June

there the absence of doves
    their non-arrival
        and footless chatter
            struck me with something

you couldn't call awe
    but a perfectly normal
        everyday openness
            touching on reverence

and there lay in the world
    a resplendent expanse as clear
        as the sun in miniscule steps
            on feet red as wine

an ever enamoured
    intricate stalking
        of food and desire
            in cavernous day

a mumbling of cravings
    second by second
        to circumvent death
            and impart a sweet nearness

it struck me that writing
    of doves or the rain
        begins in an egg
            in one giddy drop

with downy feathers
    and gathering drops
        feather by feather
            into one sought drawing

with ashen brown
    and white in blue
        pristine colours
            and water in air

with a somewhere heart
    and delicate lungs
        oxygen ferns
            the webbings of clouds

abstracted and then
    at the same time thirsting
        for a joy that is man's
            and all the attainable

words come to naught
    so utterly senseless
        so rain gets to rain
            and doves can alight

so soft on this white
    sheet of paper I
        can easily see if they write about me
            or of you

or even the rain
    or of peace through which only
        a little round eye
            peers through a blur to us

on a morning in June the day twenty-six.

Birgitta Trotzig
(Sweden)

Excerpts from *Sammenhang* (*Interrelations*)

(Threshold, boundary, dividing line, outside, inside)

Now what is the connection between art and the natural world. Where does imagination's space arise. That which is neither this. Nor that.

You can manage without what they call the **I**.

The boundary, the secret of the threshold. What is out, what is in, what is outside of me, what is inside me.

On the threshold. Not on this side, not on the other side.

Precisely in moving across the threshold. The membrane of appearances will burst. The counterfeited I that sees. It is then the world is stripped bare. Light begins to speak, stones begin to breathe. And the eye becomes a black planet, so the world now sees. Trees lift roots out of the earth, out of the soil of dead trees. Clay and the traces of man is what the blindness sees, hands of the dark, feeling your way. In the profundity of night, stellar constellations record what is fulfilled and unfulfilled.

The archer lets his arrow fly. It is deadly.

Everything speaks to everything. In the light of space, in the light of darkness. The message reveals itself.

•

the dreams of children...

.

Evil and good, darkness and light

Is the gleam of life, darkness beneath. This is a mountain village. Among the stones, bodies of the dead lying in the earth. The earth is formed by the dead. The sun in full glare, a black ring rounding it. Light skirts the water, the water streams and sings. The greying crown of the olive tree is filled with light, it stirs, wanders. The snake rests quiet in the wall's crack.

The plants of spring, birds, the mountains. Labiates by the stone well, the light. The dead in the earth are covered by shining life. The gleam of life, the pungent scent of honey and fetid excrement. Light skirts the water, the water gleams and speaks.

Faces are dug up like stones from the earth. Sun in the sky, never moving. Birds, wind, earth sucked into the burning shadow of light. Never moving is a powerful motion. The blind skin grows over the wound. Faces burst open.

The dead children sit by the wall.
They see things.
A sea is what they see. A sea of blood.

People of forewarning. A soot-blackened town behind dark clumps of melted plastic.

Standing by the roadside, those who are fleeing, each has the same kind of eyes, narrow, deep-set. Deeply engraved, deeply kept in the skull bone these eyes brighten frighteningly limpid, all too limpid water holes pure as crystal, of a kind not to be read, not to be interpreted. Wild water holes of the wild.

judgements…

History is blind. But full of traces. It is as dark as the universe, spanning time and space, consisting of eyes, living eyes of death

The ancient raw stones on the mountain stand like judges.

The only word, the only activity, the only memory. Life is transformed through and through into a judgement, an obtrusive implementation of a judgement. Every word emerges, every activity, every omission. The loose mass of lies crumbles into distinct components, distinct yeses and nos, nothing is effaced, everything has total significance

The Word created the world. The law of the Word drew the boundaries between being and not being. Thus we live now on the border.

The law makes reality visible. Without law a flickering, a teeming, the motley bloody accumulation of anonymous skins, bodies, scattered about indiscriminately, healthy and rotted, you can eat anything at all
The law makes reality
The law cuts through, violates, sculpts—it becomes a miserable shrieking state of affairs, reality being now when the face of the Messiah emerges in his death gloom. (The face of the slain Messiah, the unacknowledged inner shadow, the persecuting image of anguish, shadow image of that which has been denied)

The face of the betrayer can be beautiful, pure, impossible to interpret

The betrayer worships, loves, is humiliatingly basely unctuously and exaltingly sublimely soaringly bound to, never freeing himself of the thought of, tasting the fragrance of the skin of two realities, their different skins, different blood, different shiverings, different tremors of blessedness— one day the eschatological moment must arrive, mortally opposing realities finally blending into one indissoluble shimmering, into one unfathomably boundless corporeal gloom

"No one can serve two masters." Yet he doesn't even know who he himself is.

The soul of the betrayer glistens like the Babylonian serpent bird, shimmering in colours, iridescently multifarious— hate him you love, love him you hate, white mould under the feathers

The betrayer serves two masters, loves them both, lives within himself the life of the two realities—one day they must be locked in an insoluble struggle, at the end of the ponderous bitter road there is only murder's soulless quietude.

The betrayer is a clump of dead weight falling, falling, the weight falling into gravity's inexorable orbit; once chosen it must run its course, the seven eyes of the roman die have been cast.

The betrayer will never acknowledge that the soul of the betrayer is his own. He looks at it as were it a foreign being, an odd parasite that has taken up residence within him and sucks, from membrane and tissue, the very substance of his life, converting into itself living matter

The feet of the betrayer walks the stony way stone by stone up towards the black olive grove, its bloody darkness: bewildering torches flame about him. He can't really know who he is. Behind him, Jerusalem's steep walls—either yes or no. His feet lead him to wherever he wants and wherever he doesn't want.

After having "greatly kissed" the man he loved, thereby denouncing him.

The betrayer, a mute terror of an I disguises himself as many, flees from one person to the next. "I am Legion. For we are many." The masks speak, crying out sham utterances in sham voices. Beneath them, the bare rock base's austere silence alone.

Existence as a tortuous mine shaft down low, caged and suffocating yellow-grey light, clammy tissue heavy with sweat, dull pooling water, helpless eyes caught crossed
"after denouncing those he loved and watching them die because of him, he sat for seven days on ashes, peering into death; then death chose him for a life with it."

They who bear my guilt for me.

The forest of illness is grey. Sometimes it exudes a terrible whisper. It cannot be called a voice. Impossible to discern within it any kind of message. It is a hush, the gnawed body of that which has come to silence.

You pass among empty tumbledown houses of stone, pavilions, farms, shaft after shaft, all the ice-cold walls, half-demolished administrative buildings, culverts (collapsed, filled-in with earth) windy vacant corridors, ancient body of this earth, eyes of earth, memory's inexhaustible labyrinth plunged in darkness. Beneath the dark veil with no face, lips. They cry out to me in the night. Then they visit me in dreams. In dreams they move within my moving. The muted silence is the voice there

What the world is like. They bear my guilt for me.

The madhouse is black. Marvellous faces emerge alive from within it.

They arise from the common guilt, from the murderous viscous walls they rise as growths from something entirely foreign, organic matter, fresh and limpid, they grow from guilt as a rose from dark blood

The savage grimy serene mass of faces

The black viscous walls, the shoddy water pipes, the enamel basin that has rusted away, the three dead trees between high walls of the tiny home, stifling. The hard gravel. Within their eyes, in the black hazy well of their glances, the mountain of explanation can be seen. Out into the luminous soundless unknown they journey now on foot, ever journeying

—where does the water come from?
—the skies drive down rain, weeping life

The mountain
The life of the mountain exists that it may be destroyed.
The bare rock-face gazes out into the day, the night, the
blowing rain
The rain is darkly aglitter. It closes the earth in autumn
then opens it up in the spring. It penetrates to the very tips
of the trees' crown-shaped roots, opening the skin of men
What is the water?—maker of cracks, transformer who
dissolves away, fashions anew
Frees the stones
Gradually the naked rock gets broken down, debris
makes its presence felt, shards fall away to become gravel.
Thunder comes. Rain comes. Ever so gently the mountain,
tight as a bolt, becomes transformed, water streaming across
the rocky presence, drawing with it the crumbling moun-
tain. Now there is only earth and mud. Water trickles through
the ground, separating and disintegrating, muck and rubble,
roots and detritus flow along with the dark coursing waters
out towards a roaming sea, heaving and rising, the place of
great motion

—look how all those fragments, faceless and with faces,
are drawn together on a beach to a city. Rained to bits, shells
collect in heaps upon the soft earth, cracks in the ground
moving continually. Sand basins, pools, reeds, and a foam
congealed into brownishness, rearing up, ramparts raised
against the sea.
Houses that are white. A sea that blackens. Between shells,
walls, the warm twilight of man. A heart beat. A flickering

candle. The earth of the open land flows out into the sea. Here is the borderland where leavings accumulate, beings of the earth and of the water, the dark throbbing through them like a pulse. The intense life of dissolution. Shells that break apart. Life ever forming itself anew.

(and look how time makes its great way, weaving awesome webs of roots, inscrutably vibrant systems where each and every part has its way of growing, its particular tending movement. Human beings live as time cells within the multifarious system of a greater time. Everything there is unfathomable, mightily vaulting, driving forward, incomprehensible, inexorably metamorphosing. Fragments of skin and roots. Deeds and memories emerging and disappearing. No one can know what he is in the wild forest of time. Or how the enormous vaulting, the ever-expanding twining motion, dark and giant-like, will end. Or even if there will ever be an end to these endlessly combining motions. Look how one finds a dwelling within a context. Unfathomable and endless. One is fitted into God's inscrutability. You distinguish no more than lightning, dreams and tatters— a chasm in the midst of disjointed oppositions, much as an ancient spine of rock will emerge from the smoky light of a misting sea. Time ever growing. Ever and ever growing)

•

epiphanies…

Chinks of light, transformations. The face/the body rises out of an unknown universal space, the soul encompasses the visible being with a great blackened space, filled with a bulk of unharkened, vanished voices. Each being has an as yet unobserved universe surrounding it, within it, dark solar systems are journeying

What takes place in there? Things are hidden away within these shrouded worlds. Objects that cannot be defined, cannot touch you. Animal? Being? Something stirs without warning, as when the night, fissuring into a single distilled chink of moonlight, resembles a potsherd, a toy, an instrument, a garment. A landscape full of ruins, a face, vacant eyes, things of a life. At night, the body encounters its transformation. Unfathomable, the shower of water is heard, stones rolling over, voices always voices

Membrane gone. Concepts gone. To exist is to be singular weighted stones

—a distinctive landscape, during a heat wave a half-evaporated rill. The stone-scorched throat of the falls, mammoth boulders, blackening grey, filled with ingresses to the earth's gloom, forming a runnel through the parched forest of thorns. Watery convergences gleam black, and, beneath the stones, the resting water mirrors the rainbow-like sun. In this world of stone, the eye of the moth in metagreening green, the sun in the black lake, the sun in the black waters. An eye that is green pink blue, huge or the tiny microscopic body of the heavens—translucent through the black, the majestic sun of the end the sun down in the great yellow flowers, froth of light, the black woods behind. Light frothing, light. Black creek roaring. The two components, life and death, the smoky light of flowers, foam of a flower's sweetness, darkness, the dark shadow falls upon the garden, the nearer it is to the dead, the more intense it becomes—a bliss so intense as to turn skin itself into light, the heat of light. Being: a burning vascular network of vision through the body of the falling light. The dark of the forest breathes. Deep under the limpid rounding of the creek's black waters—in a dream the wheel of the mill turns inexorably, inexorably. Death and life speak to one another now. On the border. The border between lips and the word

Time is the green leaf's clear blood, the
fluid of transformation. It pales the leaf, with a
red color rising. From where does it come?—
this is not a sign of health. And then, time. Its
yellow already shining with the grimness of
death.

The delicate cranium of a child is a fullness of completion no other form knows. And it is like no other form in the universe. The eyelids of a child are woven into transparency. In its pupils the world moves within a mirror.

The temples of a child are yielding, with a particular kind of shade, as beneath a wing. Endless life is ever visiting there, having chosen one of its innumerable roads, channels, pathways, sub-earthly springs. There the majesty of life pulses and throbs through the parietal bone's delicate branchings, finds delimitation with the completion of its own veiny tree, the green–blue coronal's shadow upon the brown gloss of the cranium. Deep within the enclosure of the thinnest vessel, billions of labyrinths give off sounds and murmurs, voices come to life, voices come to visit, the azure light of a shimmering fish, a sloping deep within, all the way down. His ear is listening to the sounds within and to the sounds without. Lips form the perfect image of a voice. The larynx awakens the tongue now rolling towards interpreting. In the black mist of its gaze, voices are in motion. The gaze of the child is a font of astonishment

How do you cross the border

What is the borderland like

It is a road. It is snow. It is a long journey,
road after road. Left, there is a mountain,
impenetrable—to the right, downwards, down-
wards, the enormous frozen expanse of the lake's
surface widens out. Tract after tract of vast
stretches of ice, white lines alternating, venous,
solidified currents disappearing into the murky
dissolution as acid-burning winter light, more
impenetrable than the mountain, neither white
nor black. Over the ice fields unknown bodies
of light are making their way, on foot.

Willum Peder Trellund

(Denmark)

Time Between

Until the nightmare expires
from the strain of repetition
and hope is born
on the fields of exhaustion
with birds lifting from them
as one and one alone
is born out of the confusion
with wings enough to bear.

Then you will be with me
your face
big as heavens.

Portal

In a portal of stillness
there is a torch
and the portal opens its wings of blue
to the silver heavens
—and this heart, she that never was,
is as it always shall be
with one bird singing

No one knows why
that bird is singing
It is as though its wings were
prying gates apart
—all the other gates—
as though its wings
were part of the heavens,
and in every portal
there is a torch
and it is burning
—just why
no one knows.

And the book
is a gate that is open
that has nothing to do with wings
yet in its very silence
its sets an angel
free

And the book lies open
with the light reading in it
and wings that open the light
and in that opening
you can see
what is written:

An angel was sent
to those who were wise
and the wise knew nothing to say

Child

Light breathes
as spirit's breath
lightens
days wile on
in flower dust.

Down silvery roads
a child is walking
and for a long time he is marvelling,
until the street opens onto
a portico
cool and green and very still.
There are broad lawns there
filling with sun.

Colossal grown-ups
tramp around
paths of crunching gravel.

The child nears
his discovery of the world
he streaks with confidence across
the lawns, tip-toes soundlessly
—unaware
the world he treads exists
is already
discovered

It opens
before his gaze,
the child laying
the world open
as a tiger
parting foliage.

Barbarously
he moves among thickets,
unaware
the path is somehow right,
is snug,
protected,
is among
the other animals and birds

Angels
follow him
wherever he goes.

In This Setting

In a setting of silver
and gliding eyelids
and lashes never flashing
sleep out of sight,
sleep that is this setting, gliding
silvery sleep.
and the dust on these photographs
of nothing
kissing nothing
—which is this silver scene gliding
as water itself will glide
on through.

No, there is a real presence here
as in the times I see
angels of silence, intimately present,
—the drizzling rain never ceasing to caress me
far into the fever—
and the angel
is still, very still
and spreads very slowly opening wings
and in tremulous blaze
lofty in the hushed light
the angel stands
and it spreads very slowly opening wings
and in a storm
where silver-beaten fans open
into a seething mirror
the angel stands and spreads very slowly
opening wings
and in a shower of words
intones eons of silence
transforming itself into light
and the angel spreads slowly

opening wings
and the light from the wings
spreads silence in the snow
falling softly as down does
from the wings of angels
spreading light
as on the first morning
and in the wings of angels
is the light's tremor
and in the light's tremor
the silver of silence
and in the storm of silence
wings spread out angels
and they embrace you
with a light
you do not understand
but one
that understands you
and the angels spread very slowly
their opening wings
and they embrace the heavens
and it is God who sings
as he has always sung creation
and the angels surround him
with a wall of
reticence, tenderness and intimate presence
and the angels become silent
until the appointed hour.

but through eons of silence
silence is walking
like the fall of an angel's feather.

Descent

The well
a boring into
shared consciousness
ground water

A dark
glance down there
a vertical tunnel up
and from the bottom
you can see the stars
even more clearly
even in daytime

When you have gone down
all the slimy steps
and have been
caressed by the algae there
when you have become one
with the black water that is
perfectly clear
cool and pure
when you
have been born once more
have become
a child, a doll, an eye's dark pupil,
seed of knowing,
when you have become the water's
consciousness
the well's spying glass
you will in time
see
the pillar of life
in your neighbour
and in him the beginning
the child

you forgive
and see the stars
more clearly.

The Double Demon

Suddenly
the shape of his shadow
dividing on the wall behind—
each part moving
reft from the other

No dual source of light
nor play of flame flickering the wall
threw the joker's shadow before me
there was only the electrical standing lamp
naked and sober
nor was I rapturous, drunk

His shadow divided above me
lifting himself in supercilious disdain
a head of contempt, a jackal
cruel and ironic
twitching features
and the pleasure of a complacent
evil
caustic, sneering
in theatrical exactitude
—and down there, on the opposite side
dangling in a stooping gesture
the head of a child
languorous features
and an expression
devoid of spirit
as though it were
still-born
monstrous
yet through some devilish miracle
brought to life, though in torment
because of that life,

and all the while
in all that time
the face was speaking,
masked, deadened
empty, entranced, kept speaking
yet with someone else's voice
inexorably hardened,
with words that
mocked.

I was filled with a cold
crystalline silence
while I spoke to the demon,
as though the coolness of observing
provided me somehow with a transparency
that was
invulnerable
as though I were
in my inmost self
crystallized
rock

I am no longer afraid
of the fury
darkness can bring about.
I am shielded. Now.
Initiated.
Into knowing.

Love Poem

In-The-Mean-Time bursts
down the middle
and in that space
a rose
unfolds

a light beams flickering wings
breaking
the mind's
glass
house

Stony sorrow
plunges down the deepest well
waters rushing upwards
fully
rapturous

And the trees rush upwards too
brimming hymns—
never have these slopes reared so high
before a storm so wild
or love as dear

Birgitta Lillpers
(Sweden)

Green Vale

Can a wind blow in the stillness
can it blow that way
within a frozen picture
hot

The heron flies in
I wish it were to a place
emptied of memories
The heron is flying in over green glass and brown, glass
from paint shops' forgotten sloshings
for dreamt flooring,

                          pharmacies, the heron

is flying in
over willows, lilacs madly, tough
                       switches, it

flies, is flying in,
I wish
it were over a place
empty of memories, with the black
cherry-red grasp of a woman
in daytime, I would wish a heron
over an empty place
               and our skins, our
true objectives, might be lead round
their own digressions, heron
heron
           fly in.

Where is warm moderation, the time where we pause
before lapsing, you know just before the
much-too-furious skirmish
towards the inmost rib-cage.

Where is dry moderation's snug and sounding arboreal crown,
with light, water
water in round, shallow bowls where
the heron strangely fragile
is judged
only in someone else's dream and
can fly in over a garden's brown and green glass.
Where! is this warm moderation,
the fragility of the strange heron
possible

Annunciation: the angel had cracked lips, full and white

She went out with several kinds of longing
mixing strangely in her heart. The ground, everything
as if everything were taking place
under water. Above
the terrace out among the bushes in
trackless sand. She carried on
until she ran into a stranger who could shape words,
and who drew her away and held her attention
for hours.

She could explain it now:
There, hands are still.
Beyond the absence of what is still unknown
                           different from the absence
                           of what once was.

Where you are
something,
without talking about anyone else,
so that hands can be still, so that
what is within the house and what is without
can merge into a single fullness, as the
night here does, with the day,
the easily swept twenty-four hours of dream
and wakefulness,
bush gleaming the floor the sand
the waters of man:
you close the doors only
to complete the house's quadrature. The house
nonetheless retaining its nervous little chinks opening onto
revelations and a quiet within
                           nervousness.
And each object has the scent of something other than solitude,
        obliterating it.

Build a home in steely light:
life is the sixth sense.
Water flows over and
mixes, yet she is not dead.
She is beneath the surface.
All the sea
is above her.

And Bend Me Ringing Like Blades

And bend me, burned in the knowing
of that which isn't obvious

is strong in its presence
And when you grasp it
your hands will bear the scent—
propolis

And from then on you will be marked
by propolis
with nothing to save you
from this mark.
You have it as a strength
that also is
a weight.

Timid and with little ease you know
that total clarification would have been death, *and
bend me ringing like blades*, over the only sphere
of totally clarified time there is, *bend me,ringing*

like blades

Bend me ringing like blades
above the sudden nocturnal skin strewn on
your lustre,
facets to tally
from neck to
body to
body

yes *bend me ringing*
like blades

The Death of The Bumble Bees
And The Mallow Plant's Mysterious Openness
Rosy, Soft, Enraged

The mallow grows high. I stare up in all
the good wells.
Shirking that
which need be shirked. Still.
Now and then I shatter glass. It is
inevitable, with
the shards. And now
bumble bees are dying. I see myself just now
in all your eyes
prepare
to be visible. Now and then, seen,
I shatter glass. If only a bumble bee
might slumber
in the cup of such a shard,
cradle, blue.
Now the bumble bees are dying, their deaths as round
as their bodies, as though everything were moving along
just a wee more slowly
as warmth flowing the other way.

They head for certain degrees, sit
at the fork where the leaf fastens and
at right angles onto the house; when I
speak of the death of bumble bees, my
beloved then says to me *but, you know,*
they are old and tired, they have lived,
their buzzings, their sleep, calmly kneading
death, as honey and bone meal, even
in winter something stirring can emerge
from within the mixture, it is that
warmth, a leg, a pincer, and in this way
sleep quickly becomes
something else.

The mallow grows high and we don't cut the
mallow down. We stare up
in all the good wells. The children
born and unborn, have
spaces, vast stretches or black
holes. Now and then
I shatter glass. That is
the sound I bring about
through the days.

Thus it was here grasses of the darkness
were wet. We could sense it had been a reasonable
time. We burned them,
went about our lives and maintained there was a bond
between body and thought. The sound of a carafe
with water in it one night. We were being tested
after all. Knocked about
and throttled. Until we noticed we stood
firm: transformed through sheer exhaustion
and a sort of delicate
frenzy.

We don't cut the mallow plants down. We no longer wait
for a beginning. These evenings stand rumbling
stand added to in places deep in fire and among
tops of the larkspurs, bluish, black, beany nuts between
teeth, grey-green sleep, where
violence and death shower forth,
and are stared at.
Now and then I shatter
glass.
Now and then I shatter
glass.

Now

Now you will surely have to keep tabs
on the kind of frailty the dahlias really have,
how hardy they are too; you will
to your amazement
contrary to all you've heard
find an almost boundless strength (in a phase of packed pollen,
the feeling of blackest reds)
suspended
with nubs
of sustenance
and the smell
within
burst
fissures

You will have to keep closer tabs
on the course of the moon
so the moon
turning up above the barn
does not become the fierceness you require
paralysing you perhaps
with sudden absence, you
will also have to keep tabs on
how you might endure
so strong a love,
the layers of pain it embraces
are so many
you sometimes
think of it as a
kernel of pain, cobalt blue,
really cobalt blue
and it frightens you this cobalt blue—you

will really have to keep tabs
on the way you arrange
what will become
your very own
humiliations
the way you allow the things you arrange
to become
humiliations—you
really will have to keep tabs on things

Finally

Finally
in where the brightest most silent cries
bend into silenced, whitening, salting
finally in where the saltiness of whitening the hush
lies without a sound in the most silent
the whitest, upon
> the purest salt
> the hottest tile
and words are scorched away by light
and words are burned in and exist, they exist

into that which is filled
more is ever lain, and
there is room.
To the greater fullness
deeper depths
get measured
vaster wastes
stepped out, ever augmenting
new limitlessnesses of the finite,
that we may be wakeful.

And that which is despair
for the sake of the ineffable,
whitens in whitening, in
puffs of salt, flings out,
thrusts forward into the din of
blue, of red, of the scent of
propolis.
And within the white of the inmost
the heart of the inmost
is a serenely weighted fastness
a levity, rounded and dark,
and it speaks.

Stein Mehren

(Norway)

The Wind

Wind before daybreak, you are not wind, you do not
  blow, you are a wind before the wind, listening
across the earth…in breaths of light, gusting,
  gleaming in ice. As a crown of starry leaves
you blow out the heavens above this land drunk with night,
  brightening. You break from seals of the dew,
spheres within spheres, the earth beaming: Light
  over sheening spans of water, mirroring
there where birdsongs run like chinks of light, you draw
  the skies behind you, a seven-colored robe
of forest wakening within a rushing wind of five seas.
  Wind like a wind before the wind, gusted out of the light
into the circulation of waters, the open trembling of the high leaves
  As the earth itself, heaven by heaven,
rises from the sea. Like a birth. An embrace.
  Like death. Like wind. Everything that trembles in wind

Prologue

An eye. Light and its darkening.

Human consciousness is a darkening that stores the universe's
power of light

A sun shut up within a body. An eternity locked within a tiny
bit of time.

With a longing that holds the entire universe within it.
And at the same time

An image of the world rounded by space, itself
holding worlds it seeks to contain.

An endless night closed within the light, light shoved into night
like a star

A sun so at one with itself as to be inseparable from the glance
that would see it

An eye. A darkening and its light.

Sun Boat

In those times we called one another the high names of strange gods and the barn was a boat of the sun that would soon set forth, the warm breath of the farm animals, rapturous sun in the hay of the heat of sleep, heat of grains, heat of growing. And beneath, the cowshed, within the barn's deeper self, as if within the belly of a Cosmic Mother. With the cowshed's floor as an open lane, steaming. Everything was perfectly still. Yet we could sense the animals, growing things, the heavenly bodies, and our bodies trembled.

Remember? There was night upon the land. The grownups called it war. And we were the children of the war. Sent here because our parents were frightened. The barn was the castle of death. In autumn storms, when the wind slammed the doors and the walls were a chattering sheath the summer shed in its flight from its slough. Suddenly the door would burst open. Deep within the fire we could make out the salamander. The war. I can still see my childhood in there, sparking with flames, in the fire zones of memory.

I've met you since then. You smiled as if I still loved you. But it isn't you I want back. It is my childhood... You had to avenge yourself and say: the human brain is a computer. And soon we will have computers that can think, dream, write poetry. All by themselves. I smiled and said: But that is a memory that has neither gender nor childhood... And suddenly the salamander emerges between us. It is as though I were in the barn again. My fingers trace the pattern in the wood and your face begins to shine through. And you have stars all the way down to your eyelids. The growing things, the animals, the heavenly bodies.

Once the barn was the whole world. One with the universe. Childhood's hay-loft, gleaming walls, galleries of the sun, light like silk and brocade. I don't know why I think of great ships that have sunk in time to the bottom. Sunken deep within the sex of the earth I float desultorily flowing in dreams...I lay within the belly of some huge animal, deep within the brute in him, not yet human. Even in the middle of winter, summer wind gusted through the barn, through the hay, where light sinks to the bottom of itself and the hay glows fiercely from out of the summer's rapture.

Childhood's perilous enchantment, entangled in a web of parental love. Like imagos in cocoons of fear and warm contentment. We tore ourselves out of childhood, casting ourselves into each another, so that we might sink to the bottom of one another. It was like allowing heaven and earth to perish in the depths so that they might find a new heaven, a new earth. I remember our childish hugging, even more keenly than I remember us, and the barn as a mire we got stuck in, surviving. Can you remember the animals? Huge glossy animals huffing and puffing, moving like summer magnets somewhere in the darkness. Life streaming in circles of flame behind the vaporous sweaty hides of life. Spring breezes in light gusts through the walls into our blood. Your face, the lead of a family medallion, in a deep space of gray light.

At that very moment the door burst open and a gust of wind blew in from the naked field...mixing the cowshed's hot breath into a blue veil of twilight. Remember how we lay, like two people trying to discern the meaning of stars, as we gazed through the transparencies of our bodies, opening each other up into our own personal orbits. And suddenly, the heat of the cowshed flowing over our limbs and we knew that we bore the summer as a rapturous sun, deep within ourselves and our hearts stamped like beasts in the rooms of desire.

We survive within what is brutish. Remember we dressed up as animals, a Christmas billy-goat and a scarecrow. A game that never knew any end. At night we were swaying through dreams over houses, field and hill, in the apparel of animals. We knew we had to get out of it and be human again. I wake at night even now, above my own face. It isn't life that dies. It is we who die. Winds, hills, the earth, trees, grasses, the light, are all the same. What is it there that dies? Disappearing so deeply down in sleep and oblivion that it emerges again as what is remembered, as eternity and desire.

I have returned. It is evening. An evening suddenly illumining, a glint from some long absence. The air cleared and wet, rain-light among the thickets. It was as though time himself were trying to make himself eternal in us. I open the door, a door to my own remembering. I can sense the hay, the heat of the earth, flowing into the empty cowshed, light glaring fantastically. Someone comes to close the door of the cowshed. A person in the opening of light. I can discern the salamander. It flares up suddenly with a thread of light around it and it becomes human again. I think I can see your face as an open door. The growing things, the animals, the heavenly bodies. In your face, you step out of your gender and I see all the way across death…

Once, a long time ago, you were me. Once, a long time ago, I was you. We called each other the high names of strange gods.

Sirens in December

Tracts of ice. Chiming. Steel and crystal
     As a cry above the terrified deep
Thus water reveals
          its cosmic kinship
Locked within a hollow armored chest
               of singing frost
it acquires the clarity of star clusters

Mom's face in the sky. And the word
   "arrested". A non-word from the darkening
bomb shelter of my childhood. Sirens
and window panes in an exploding living room: an ice-star
    I can remember scarcely more than
      the terror of grownups. But the war
was mine, like a cry across the ice plains.

Steely nights. Ice-stars. Life and death
    are bound as deep as beaten iron. Darkness swills on
      through us as water and ice
           on the starless deep
Through plains of ice, I see the river flowing still
  black and transparent
     among reeds beneath the waters, level
above a face much like my own

From the dark room of memories, he whose father
  came from the wrong side of the war, was that why
we made him eat a live rat
   I am sitting in the air-raid shelter
    of forgetting
face to face, with myself
   like pictures there below the ice, in dark flowing water

The Love of A Woman

It wasn't his sex, but his childhood
she would have within her. Hounded into some place where
there would be no other choice but her, her. No mere reflection
no, the mirror itself, not his approval, but the cry of the birthing child
is what she would have, his first and last word in the world.
She would have him wail most bitterly in her name,
force his way into a sun
                    he was to remember nothing but that

With the same hand that would grasp a star, he was
to grasp her, his very being broiling
within his clasping arms. Here, right here, in *this* world!
In picture after picture he was meant to discover: Her.
Much as the sun might, night after night, discover a moon, pale and
ineluctably still. Should he wish to flee, she was to be the path of his
flight and he was to approach her from all directions, strong
        as one who would place a dream upon the heavens: Her!

She would not caress but rather flail him, as a cleft
in the quaking earth. She was to be the only crevice in the wall of
despair, the only place he could possibly plant
his desire…she would know the taste of death within him.
The trapdoor of memory. Rent seams of common sense
and dreams. She knew where she had him, yet others
had had him before. She would send crashing all time within him,
twisting it out of shape, so he would
                    have to pick up from the beginning—with her

For she knew him right down to the faces that lay beneath his skin,
down to her finger tips, and as to his former life, his caresses gave
him away. When he breathed heavily beside her, she could hear
moans and whimperings of other women…ravenous, she would
follow the trail, devouring it, she would have him…lose his mind, all
the better to love him on down into a love he had either forgot
or dreamt. There where he would lose himself totally—there where
he would be split open, surrendering himself completely
                    There, is where she would, *have*, him…

Corona II

The elements dreaming us from this darkness to the next
Earth-dreamt Wind-dreamt Water-dreamt Fire-dreamt, when it
comes to the infinity of universal space it is like a needly eye
we just have to get through

Space and Time and Freedom. Get to know these concepts through
and through, just how they contort. Under great pressure,
the interior of darkness swinging into light. Wind-dreamt is night
a black hole that permits no seeping light

Earth-dreamt is death. Life within a crystal of terror
Horizons hell-bent on collapsing. A feathered explosion of bird
in a body of light, your narrow splinter of night. Fire-dreamt

Fire-dreamt is frost. Confluent beams of icy light years of space
we see the light of creation before it becomes
resurrection's light. In that darkness breaks into it,

We are Water-dreamt. Heavenly bodies wrapped in darkness, we
break into death and it is there we love. Within the speed of light
it is always midnight. Fire-dreamt. Know nothing dead

Heavenly plains of the casting light. Ice-stars colliding
    with them. The shadows of sirens crossing faces
        Light years dividing the day from the night, life from death
Light years crashing suddenly through us

Epilogue

At the bottom of the light's well there is a dark star. Like a shriek surrounded by living light.

In the darkroom of memories the sun of remembrance is born.

What we as children were allowed to see, but couldn't be bothered to see and thus forgot, are blind spots within us. These are what enable us to see.

The flat crust of a wound that has become an eye

A sunken childhood, a buried past that becomes an eye in a dream

What within you has not allowed itself to be rankled. Or destroyed. That which is of love.

The flat crust of a wound that has gained vision

The blind in us that sees

That which is not spoken, that sees

Between the lines, that which is said within what has not been said

The vanishing point on the horizon of expectation

The point of emergence on the horizon of vanishings.

The relation between that which sees itself in us and that which shapes us without seeing us.

At the bottom of the night's well there is a star of light.

The Poet Praises the Language

The poet praises the language, admitting he doesn't
understand how any language can find its way into us
divided as they are into classes, declensions, three genders
Blinded, perforated, bodiless, spoken to death-
subsisting alone from that which no word can hold
we find, within the language, the remains of a dead language
Words that rose and vanished, in darkness so near
one another they merge into everything we say.
The longings of the dead are very much alive. Speaking ever in us.
Do not near them… That which never let itself be tamed
will not now be tamed. We board the frail vessels words
are, sailing to the world's end to find the one word that would
render all words superfluous. We tremble behind bars of
complaint, entreating common sense to watch over us. Yet it is
the abyss that safeguards our life. On the far side of words there
is a poem writing us. The poem we should have lived.
In *that* poem we bear the blame for everything that has
been said from the moment man began to speak
In this way we bear the blame for the bruised words
in every cry…the blame for the superficiality
of words flooding conversations. In all we say
we are responsible for the final human's final words.

The Summer House

Every autumn we leave something of ourselves
in the summer house. For two days we straighten things up,
then we give in, tossing our junk into
drawers and cupboards, lock the door and walk away
from the house that lies now like a hushed beacon
We come back a few times in the winter
breaking into the dozing locked-down space
breathy in the membranous light. There is the cry of a bird
and faint smells of the lake in the hallway,
the vibrant light of the sea
washing steps, these things dream their own life
encased in a sun-warmed sheath of shadows
projected in restive images over the walls and roof
The last one to lock up must have left his shadow
somewhere behind the blind, dark, doomed roads
And the spaces we left behind us resemble in our memories
the whispering sweep of the sea. High-ceilinged skies
like the day spring arrives and we open the locked door
knowing the spring's own summer, its puffs of wind
gusting towards us

Didda
(Iceland)

Iceland's Honour

Me on board a trawler.
From Greenland.
Completely lushed
from spirits and beer.
My arms and legs just about holding on,
one turn to the side from crashing out.
The Faeroese was trying to tell
the Greenlanders I was a nice person.
They just laughed and pinched me.
There were at least two I had bunked with
but they were Danes.
So the Greenlanders kept on
marking me with bruises, thumping
me heartily on the shoulders.
And there I sat with them,
sang a song, and there was the whispering
of "jeg elsker dig" by many kinds of voices.
And I felt like a fish factory girl
gutting away, up to my crotch in roe.
I tried to gather all the inferiority complexes
we small nations have into one, but the only
thing I felt was this active empathy
and fathomless interest in the effects of firewater.
They'd already started working up on deck,
so I put myself ashore with three
stolen beer bottles in my coat pocket.
And the lads at the landing bay laughed
and said something and I told them
to shut their mouths.
Me a trawler whore? NO!
I am the sword of Iceland, it's shield and honour, staggering
off into Tryggvagata.

The Never Never Scar

We were never beaten. And nor was she. Even though he broke his own arm hitting her. So that what I remember is just real nightmares. I was beaten. But not us. And certainly not her. I was beaten because I caused trouble, unless that was my imagination too. Once when I had done something which I can't even remember, he treated me differently.

He dragged me up to my room and all the way up the stairs he threatened me until my stomach sank all the way down to my knees where it trembled and shook. Then he closed the door and pulled me over his knee, putting his foot up on my bed, pulled my trousers down almost below the buttocks and slapped and slapped so the smacks echoed through the room, mixing with the shouts and screams from my throat.

I was choking. I was so angry. And my sobbing threats made him smile as he darted out, holding the door to stop me from getting at him. It would be so nice to believe that it hadn't happened. That I hadn't heard him groaning while he did it. Maybe I was difficult to hold down I don't know. That I hadn't been so afraid, that I hadn't been so angry and that the humiliation had never ever happened.

But she was never beaten. Not even when dinner was smeared on her hair and scraps were hanging all over her sweater. She wasn't beaten or called a whore and us, bastards. Not even when she had the police take him away or when she cried and cried and it was impossible to make contact with her and she pushed us away. It hadn't happened. Except that I'd caused trouble.

I staged a suicide when I was ten. Swallowed all the pills I had the guts to take, including the cat's contraceptive pill. Then I went to the cupboard under the sink and got myself a flask of Cleanol, green Cleanol, and drank it. Then I lay down on the kitchen floor beside the note I had written her where there was also a drawing of her reaction to my untimely death. I lay there and cried backwards, the tears flowing into my ears. And I waited and waited. Then I remember myself in the rubbish bin, spewing up froth and slime. Again and again. So that I thought my face would be ripped away from me.

When I told her about this many years later, she scolded me because I had been looking after my brother that evening. And what would have happened to him if I had succeeded! So the fact that she was never beaten applies to my entire pain too. It never existed.

I also staged an attack of appendicitis. And I was so successful I was sent to hospital where it was removed. Really I was hoping I would become seriously ill and could say goodbye to her and forgive her on my death bed. But I walked out of the hospital with a scar, and I still have it.

Passion

I am never above suspicion.
I am the centrifugal force of the unexpected.
I am the passion daughter of waking and dreaming.
I am Little Red Riding Hood entering the forest again and again.
Sleeping Beauty slumbering away century after a century, dreaming
never wishing to awaken.
I am reality and existence and my sisters' sorrow and joy
They sing with me when we feel the urge.
I am electricity in light and in the electric chair as well.
I am unspoken yet yelling bloody murder.
I am faith in hope and hope in faith.
I am prosaic yet rhyming all things.
Rich in nothing, full of everything,
I empty and I fill.
I am my own opposition,
daring all and hiding everywhere.
I am good when I am bad and worse when I am at my best.
Life in life and death in death.
I am written and I am told,
played and read,
painted and explained.
I am requested when everyone will have more.
My father loves me and even dares to say so outloud.
My mother finds me within her and on her and she believes in me.
I am a perfect child, a bastard,
a love child, unintentional.
I am an accident.

I am organised chaos.

I am long-desired.

I am all of a sudden.

I am the liberator of the mind from the heart.

I am flaming water and soaking fire.

I am what you are and what you do not wish to be.

I am consonance with dissonance.

I speak when silence is demanded.

I am silent when answers are required.

I am bent and also straight.

I am the knife in the wound,
the core of things.

I am the tear in the heart and the leit motif of the limbs.

I am the body inside and out.

I am all he desires but cannot understand in words.

I am the sucking drain of day and the breezing fair wind of night.

I am with you when you leave and with you when you come.

I am open at both ends but close up as soon as everything
goes out of me.

I have never died and have never been born.

I believe in you yet you always lose.

I am the only one who can hear you think, forcing you
to tell even against your will.

I am the spirit in the blood, the spirit in the wine.

I am a poison storing up and consuming.

I am the bite in the knife.

The cry from the wound.

The umbilical cord.

The last straw.

The most obvious and least visible to you alone.

I am passion.
True love of all dreams.
The power in all streams.
I am and have to be, so that
all that is may become nothing.
So that nothing may become something all by itself.

Poets and Renderers

Katarina Frostenson (1953-) lives in Stockholm. Her poetic work extends over ten or so volumes. Her monodramas have been produced on the stage and broadcast as radio plays in many countries. She has written the libretto of an opera (*The City*) by the Swedish composer Sven-David Sandström. A number of prizes have come her way, including the Swedish Academy's Bellman Prize and she has been twice nominated for the Nordic Council's Literature Prize. Her poetic world reveals itself through a mosaic of poetic shards. Poems are crafted with words she has permitted into her poetic treasure trove. They become pieces in an ever-shifting puzzle as new poems are constantly created, the process continuing on through a succession of poetry collections. She is a member of the Swedish Academy.

Lene Henningsen (1967-) Her works include seven collections of poetry, each of which reflects a natural poetic talent. Touching the air with her eyes closed, she begins to open them, adapts to the light, makes note of the emerging forms. In addition to poetry she has written lyric drama. She is the recipient of the Claus Rifbjerg Debutant Prize For Poets (awarded by the Danish Academy) and the Danish Writer's Union's Emil Aarestrup Medal. She lives in Copenhagen.

Einar Mar Gudmundsson (1954-) Translated into many languages, he is perhaps Iceland's best-known writer. He has written novels and short stories in addition to poetry, is in fact less known as a poet than as a novelist. Numerous awards have been bestowed upon him including the Nordic Council's Prize for Literature. His work is resolutely life-affirming and he peers into the darkness with little trepidation. He lives in Reykjavik, that small place teeming with writers, musicians and late night discussions of ferocious intensity.

Inger Christensen (1935-) Denmark's most celebrated poet of the day. To the delight of her readers she is finally being discovered by the non-Danish world, with translations into various languages, including English. Born in the seaside town of Vejle on the mainland of Jutland, she has lived in Copenhagen for many years. Her works include several collections of poetry, drama and radio plays (a literary form still very much alive in Germany and Scandinavia). She is the author of a number of prize-winning essays on poetry and the arts. Inger Christensen is also a translator of writers into Danish, including Birgitta Trotzig who also appears in this volume. Her poetic work is characteristically elaborated through various *systems*, mathematical sometimes or poetic (a circle of sonnets). And she has a marvellous ear.

Birgitta Trotzig (1929-) Deep and full of truth. She lives in the old university town of Lund, in southern Sweden. She has published a number of what might be described as poetic novels. Though she is a member of the Swedish Academy and respected in her own country as a writer of the highest order and though she has been translated into a number of languages, she has never before been translated into English. Why this should be is a mystery. She is the recipient of various awards including the Selma Lagerlöf Prize for Literature and the Gerard Bonniers Prize. The book from which the selections here have been made, *Sammanhang Material*, was nominated for the Nordic Council's Literature Prize.

Willum Peder Trellund (1944-) is one of the few true wielders of poetic fire in Denmark. His poetry is that of a man who has truly been through heaven and hell and survived both. To hear him read can be a life-testing experience. He simply lives and breathes poetry. If you want to meet him you have to visit his pub. There he will greet you with warmth and intensity, no matter who you are.

Birgitta Lillpers (1958-) Born and raised in Orsa, Sweden, in the rolling countryside to the north of Stockholm (Dalarna), she lives in the house of her birth. She is the author of several books of poetry as well as novels. Her poetry haunts you for days after you have heard her read it, a musical experience no one is likely to forget. She is the recipient of Aftonbladet's Literature Prize and Restaurang Prinsens Prize for Literature. Hers is a gentle way of reflecting. One imagines her standing alone on a field in Sweden, listening...

Stein Mehren (1935-) Lives in Oslo, Norway. He is the author of over twenty poetry collections and is an accomplished essayist. After living for a year in Denmark, he took up painting, an enterprise he often combines with poetry. He is no "post-modernist" relativist. No fan of the arid terrain of semiotics. He is a born poet whose poems sing of love and he is not afraid of pointing out the real enemies of mankind, those things that are inhuman, cold, of the beast. Several of his published books combine his paintings with his poems. A clear and forceful head living side by side storms of the heart. He is the recipient of numerous awards, including the Norwegian Academy's Literature Prize.

Didda (1964-) Born in Selfoss, Iceland, she grew up in Reykjavik where she now lives. She has written some poetry and two novels, both of which have caused quite a stir in Iceland, for their bare honesty. She is seen as a fiery speaker of the truth, a shatterer of false images. She has collaborated with a number of Icelandic singers (including her friend Björk), most recently Magga Stina. She has travelled to various European countries to read her work, sometimes with music, sometimes alone.

Bernard Scudder (1955-) is a distinguished translator of Icelandic into English. He has translated old things, like *Eigil's Saga* and the *Voluspa* (The Prophecy) and new things, Thor Vilmjamsson's novel, *Justice Undone* and Einar Mar Gudmundsson's *Angels of the Universe* as well as a number of Icelandic poets. He was short-listed for the Aristeon Literary Award in 1999. Born in Canterbury, England, he somehow found his way to Iceland in 1977 and has lived there ever since.

Gordon Walmsley (1949-) lives in Copenhagen, Denmark. His most recent collection of poetry is *Terebinthos* (Salmon, 1999).